A prayer, in its simplest definition, is merely a wish turned heavenward.

Phillips Brooks

Other books in the *"Language of"* Series...

Blue Mountain Arts®

The Language of Courage and Inner Strength

The Language of Friendship

The Language of Happiness

The Language of Love

The Language of Marriage

The Language of Positive Thinking

The Language of Recovery

The Language of Success

The Language of Teaching

The Language of Teenagers

Thoughts to Share with a Wonderful Mother

Thoughts to Share with a Wonderful Father

Thoughts to Share with a Wonderful Son

Thoughts to Share with a Wonderful Daughter

It's Great to Have a Brother like You

It's Great to Have a Sister like You

☆

The Language of

PRAYER

A Blue Mountain Arts® Collection

Blue Mountain Press ®

SPS Studios, Inc., Boulder, Colorado

Library of Congress Catalog Card Number: 00-029681
ISBN: 1-58786-002-3

ACKNOWLEDGMENTS appear on page 48.

Certain trademarks are used under license.

Manufactured in Thailand
First Printing: April 2000

 This book is printed on recycled paper.

Library of Congress Cataloging-in-Publication Data

The language of prayer : a Blue Mountain Arts collection.
        p.   cm.
    ISBN 1-58786-002-3 (alk. paper)
     1. Religion--Quotations, maxims, etc. 2. Spiritual life--Quotations, maxims, etc. I.
    SPS Studios (Firm)

    PN6084.R3.L36   2000
    291.4'3--dc21
                                                                                00-029681
                                                                                CIP

SPS Studios, Inc.
P.O. Box 4549, Boulder, Colorado 80306

Contents

(Authors listed in order of first appearance)

Prayer is so simple.
It is like quietly opening a door
And slipping into
The very presence of God.
There, in the stillness,
To listen for His voice,
Perhaps in petition
Or only to listen,
It matters not.
Just to be there,
In His presence,
Is prayer.

 Anonymous

More things are wrought by prayer
Than this world dreams of.

Alfred, Lord Tennyson

What It Means
to Have Prayer in Your Life

Having prayer in your life means that you have peace and comfort in your heart as you walk down any pathway your life has to offer.

It means you can talk to a caring and compassionate Father who always has the time to listen and who never fails to understand the depths of your soul.

Having prayer in your life means having the assurance that nothing can ever come your way, which you and God, united together, cannot deal with and ultimately overcome. He has His hand in everything, and things will always work out for your good.

When you pray, you can be assured, with no uncertainty, that you will be given the strength to endure anything that happens to you, and you will become a better person.

 Cathy Beddow Keener

Through prayer...
God quenches our thirsty souls,
revives our parched hearts,
and leads us to a higher place
where peace and joy and love
will be ours forever.

Linda E. Knight

Do Not Be Afraid to Come to the Lord in Prayer

There is no sorrow
   God is not aware of;
There is no valley
   where He does not dwell.
God is journeying with you always.
Moment by moment,
   trust Him completely.
Memory by memory,
   fill your thoughts with His faithfulness.
Day by day,
   rest quietly in His love.

Linda E. Knight

Have you heard God's voice?
At the same time you are searching for God,
He is speaking to you.

Billy Graham

I had learned many years ago to release my problems to God, something I had to do often in all our political years when I was trying to do so many different things at once. "Here it is, God. You take it. I can't handle it alone," I would say. It helped me through the good times and the bad. I knew that God loved me. I had found God's love a shield around me in the midst of controversy or letdowns.

☆ Rosalynn Carter

Prayer is a golden key
which should unlock the morning
and lock up the evening.

☆ John Henry Hopkins

Eyes raised toward Heaven are
always beautiful, whatever they be.

☆ Joseph Joubert

The Language of Prayer

Met a man today. Man I had seen many times before. Just sitting. With his legs crossed, hands knotted together, head hanging, hat down, and collar up. A daily fixture on the stone bench across from the children's fountain on the town green. Asleep, I think. But his lips are moving — very carefully moving. An ordinary average-middle kind of man. Size, age, clothes, condition — all ordinary average-middle. From one to two each day he sat — undisturbed by dogs, children, buses, laughter, rain, or cold. He sat. Saying something to himself, maybe. Daily.

So I asked him. One day I had to ask him. Asked him was he all right (which meant, "what's going on, buddy?").

And you know what he said? Said he was praying. Praying. Not that praying is so strange, but he said he was praying the alphabet. Just reciting the alphabet over and over for an hour each day, leaving it to Almighty God to arrange the letters into the proper words of a proper prayer. What was missing in words, he said, he made up for in fervor. He figured God could handle it and would understand.

Robert Fulghum

Prayer does not change God,
but changes him who prays.

Sören Kierkegaard

Do Your Best,
and Leave the Rest to God

Find your strength. Search for that smile of yours that makes everything brighter. Hang in there. Have faith.

Don't give up. Make a commitment... between your determination, your hopes, and your heart... that your sun *is* going to shine in the sky.

Find your way through the days with the light that shines within you. Leave a smile where there wasn't one before. Help a hurt; make it mend. Find the strength to make things right again.

Go forward, from one steppingstone to another. Reach out a little farther. Listen a little more often to what your heart has to say. Do the things that are important to you.

Make today everything you dreamed it could be. Don't settle for less; don't accept what you should not. Use the precious hours you've been given as wisely as you can. Then do your best,
and leave the rest
to God.

 Chris Gallatin

Develop the Habit of Prayer

Help me to cultivate the habit of prayer. Enable me to know Thy will. I pray that I may conform my impulses to its demands. I will pray with concentration of my mind and I will pray with all my soul. I will pray to Thee in words of devotion with all my heart and I will pray to Thee aloud and I will pray to Thee in silence, for Thou dost hear my prayers even in thought. Thou dost read my thoughts and measure my feelings and know my aspirations. I will pray that prayer may lift me to Thee and make me Thine.

Zoroastrian Prayer

We need to learn ways of praying which are compatible with the maturing of our minds and our faith.... No one should be content to remain at one level in the life of prayer nor should we abandon prayer even when... prayer seems impossible. When we do not know how or what to pray, this too, should be part of our prayer.

Perry Le Fevre

Be not forgetful of prayer. Every time you pray, if your prayer is sincere, there will be new feeling and new meaning in it, which will give you fresh courage, and you will understand that prayer is an education.

Fyodor Dostoyevsky

Pray in the early morning
    For grace throughout the day;
We know not what temptations
    And trials may cross our way.

Pray in the gladsome noontide,
    When the day is at its best;
Pray when the night o'ertakes thee
    To Him who giveth rest.

Pray in the silent midnight,
    If wakeful hours be thine;
Pray for a heart submissive,
    That never will repine.

Pray in the hour of sorrow,
    Pray in the hour of grief;
In coming to the Father,
    Thy soul shall find relief....

Pray for the Father's guidance
    In all thy work and ways,
So shall thy days be fruitful,
    Thy life be full of praise.

 Irene Arnold

Start Every Day with Prayer

When we know in our hearts that there is a God, the Father of all creation, someone who knows all things and is on our side, it is so natural to want to commune with Him every day... in praise and thankfulness, requesting help and direction for our lives and for those we love.

The repetition of starting each day with prayer helps us decide where we're going, what we want to accomplish, and how we can reach our goals. Prayer quiets our souls, makes us feel centered, and opens the door to getting our needs met. When we look to God as our provider and caregiver, we know we can go to Him boldly with our prayer requests and expect an audience with a compassionate and loving Father. Through our daily prayers, we learn to trust that God wants to supply our needs and give us the desires of our hearts. For what father doesn't want the best for his children?

When we speak our words to God with thanksgiving and release them with the faith that our requests will be granted, we put ourselves in a position to receive. God does not change and nature's laws are absolute and impartial. Thus, prayer has the potential for changing us. It connects us with God's spirit, and it is the key to His kingdom. Whatever your religious persuasion, it's a good thing to start every day with prayer.

☆ Donna Fargo

Morning Prayers...

I reverently speak in the presence of the Great Parent God: I pray that this day, the whole day, as a child of God, I may not be taken hold of by my own desire, but show forth the divine glory by living a life of creativeness, which shows forth the true individual.

Shinto Prayer

In the morning, O Lord, you hear my voice;
in the morning I lay my requests before you
and wait in expectation.

Psalm 5:3 (NIV)

Lord, the newness of this day
Calls me to an untried way:
Let me gladly take the road,
Give me strength to bear my load,
Thou my guide and helper be —
I will travel through
with Thee.

Henry van Dyke

Rising this morning
I noticed that God
Laid the world at my feet.

Corrine De Winter

Talk to God...

Communion with God is a great sea that fits every bend in the shore of human need.

Harry Emerson Fosdick

My way of communicating with God as a boy (and often even now) was through the lyrics of a song....

So I didn't have the problem some people do who say, "I don't know how to pray." I used the songs to communicate with God....

To me, songs were the telephone to heaven, and I tied up the line quite a bit.

Johnny Cash

Prayer... establishes a relationship of creature to Creator, son to Father, between ourselves and God....

Primarily, prayer is an elevating of the soul; by nature, it is converse with God; its purpose is to offer a testimonial of praise, thanksgiving, and dependence to the divine holiness, power, goodness, and mercy.

Louis Colin, C.SS.R.

A conversation with God has a way
of putting things in perspective.
He often helps us change our attitude,
find a solution, or see the humor.
God shows us what our talents
and gifts are
and how to put them to use for our
success and peace of mind.
God reminds us that mistakes and failures
are okay;
He helps us learn from them and gives us
the confidence to go on.

Life can be tough with all its challenges
and problems —
we get tired and fed up, and sometimes
we feel overwhelmed —
but it really isn't all that difficult
when you have God...
That's when life is as simple
as a prayer.

 Barbara Cage

No man ever prayed without learning something.

Ralph Waldo Emerson

Tell God Your Needs...

Don't worry about anything; instead, pray about everything. Tell God what you need, and thank him for all he has done. If you do this, you will experience God's peace, which is far more wonderful than the human mind can understand.

Philippians 4:6-7 (NLT)

When you pray, go into your room, and when you have shut your door, pray to your Father who is in the secret place; and your Father who sees in secret will reward you openly....

For your Father knows the things you have need of before you ask Him.

Matthew 6:6, 8 (NKJV)

Do what you can do
and pray for what you cannot yet do.

St. Augustine

God, give me back the simple faith
    that I so long have clung to,
My simple faith in peace and hope,
    in loveliness and light —
Because without this faith of mine,
    the rhythms I have sung to
Become as empty as the sky upon a starless night.

God, let me feel that right is right,
    that reason dwells with reason,
And let me feel that something grows
    whenever there is rain —
And let me sense that splendid truth
    that season follows season,
And let me dare to dream
    that there is tenderness in pain.

God, give me back my simple faith
    because my soul is straying
Away from all the little creeds
    that I so long have known;
Oh, answer me while still I have
    at least the strength for praying,
For if the prayer dies from my heart
    I will be quite alone.

Margaret E. Sangster

Trust in your faith,
and know that because of it,
you will receive answers
to your prayers.

Susan Hickman Sater

God is BEFORE Me,
   He will be My Guide;
God is BEHIND Me,
   No ill can Betide;
God is BESIDE Me,
   To Comfort and Cheer;
God is AROUND Me,
   So Why Should I Fear?

Anonymous

It's hard for us to accept the fact that our priorities are not the same as God's. We attach too much importance to things like popularity, wealth, and political success. To Him problems that often seem most important to us at the time are really not very significant. But God trusts us to make the best use of the time we have... and to make our lives meaningful and beneficial to others no matter where we are.

Jimmy Carter

I have learned to thank God for answering some of my prayers with "no" or "not now."

Anonymous

How gracious he will be when you cry for help! As soon as he hears, he will answer you.

Isaiah 30:19 (NIV)

Pray for a Better You

Prayer begins where human capacity ends.

Norman Vincent Peale

Incline us, O God! to think humbly of ourselves, to be saved only in the examination of our own conduct, to consider our fellow-creatures with kindness, and to judge of all they say and do with the charity which we would desire from them ourselves.

Jane Austen

Teach me to feel another's woe,
To hide the fault I see;
That mercy I to others show,
That mercy show to me.

Alexander Pope

I will not pray that each day be a perfect day, but I will pray to lapse not into indifference. I will not pray that each time I shall build both strong and true; but imperfect, I will pray for impulse that I may build anew.

Elbert Hubbard

My prayers seem to be more of an attitude than anything else. I indulge in very little lip service, but ask the Great Creator silently, daily, and often many times a day, to permit me to speak to Him through the three great Kingdoms of the world which He has created — the animal, mineral, and vegetable Kingdoms — to understand their relations to each other, and our relations to them and to the Great God Who made all of us. I ask Him daily and often momently to give me wisdom, understanding, and bodily strength to do His will; hence I am asking and receiving all the time.

☆ George Washington Carver

O Holy Spirit, descend plentifully into my heart. Enlighten the dark corners of this neglected dwelling and scatter there Thy cheerful beams.

☆ St. Augustine

I pray thee, O God, that I may be beautiful within.

☆ Socrates

Prayer Is...

...the contemplation of the facts of life
from the highest point of view.

Ralph Waldo Emerson

...to religion what thinking is to philosophy.

Novalis

...the burden of a sigh,
The falling of a tear,
The upward glancing of an eye,
When none but God is near.

James Montgomery

...believing in something bigger than yourself, or anything
you've ever touched or known. It's telling a river or an
open field that you need a little help.

Ashley Rice

...not conquering God's reluctance, but taking
hold of God's willingness.

Phillips Brooks

...impressive and powerful utterances of the heart.

Louis Colin, C.SS.R.

...the mortar that holds our house together.

St. Theresa of Ávila

...a wish turned heavenward.

Phillips Brooks

...the peace of our spirit, the stillness of our
thoughts, the evenness of our recollection, the
seat of our meditation, the rest of our cares,
and the calm of our tempest.

Jeremy Taylor

...conversation and colloquy with God.

St. Gregory of Nyssa

Prayer covers the whole of a man's life. There is no thought, feeling, yearning, or desire... which, if it affects our real interest or happiness, we may not lay before God and be sure of his sympathy. His nature is such that our often coming does not tire him. The whole burden of the whole life of every man may be rolled on to God and not weary him, though it has wearied the man.

Henry Ward Beecher

Certain thoughts are prayers. There are moments when, whatever be the attitude of the body, the soul is on its knees.

Victor Hugo

We know that all things work together for good to them that love God.

Romans 8:28 (KJV)

God Gave Us One Another

God gave us the seasons —
> each with its own beauty and reason,
>> each meant to bring us a blessing,
>>> a joy, and a feeling of love.

God gave us the sunshine,
> the rainbows and the rain,
>> the beauty and freedom of nature
to teach us the wisdom of gentle acceptance.

God gave us miracles
> in our hearts and lives,
>> little things that happen
>>> to remind us we're alive.

God gave us the ability
> to face each new day
>> with courage, wisdom,
>>> and a smile from knowing
that whatever sorrow or pain we face,
> He abides with us
>> securely in our hearts.

Most of all, God gave us one another
> to teach us about love
>> and guide us through this world,
always available to help us forward
> toward a greater understanding
>> and a greater sharing and giving
of love.

Regina Hill

God Bless Mothers...

Lord, Thou hast known
    A Mother's love and tender care:
And Thou wilt hear, while for my own
    Mother most dear, I make this prayer.

Protect her life, I pray,
    Who gave the gift of life to me;
And may she know, from day to day,
    The deepening glow of Life that comes from Thee.

As once upon her breast
    Fearless and well content I lay,
So let her heart, on Thee at rest,
    Feel fears depart and troubles fade away.

Ah, hold her by the hand,
    As once her hand held mine;
And though she may not understand
    Life's winding way, lead her in Peace divine.

I cannot pay my debt
    For all the love that she has given;
But Thou, Love's Lord, wilt not forget
    Her due reward, — bless her in Earth and Heaven.

Henry van Dyke

...and Fathers

Father in heaven, I thank You for my father on earth.
He is one of the greatest gifts You have ever given me.
And I come to You this day to ask You to bless him
in a special way,
and to ask for Your continued care throughout his life.
Keep my father safe from harm and grant him a healthy life.
You alone know how much he means to me
and all who know and love him.
Bless his efforts with success and continue to reward
his hardworking spirit.
Give him days filled with happiness, laughter, contentment,
sunshine, and beauty.
Give him the great joy of family times —
moments to be treasured forever
and memories that will never fade.
Bless him with the gift of friends who will share whatever may come,
the good times and the bad.
And above all these other things, help him to always look to You
for true peace, joy, comfort, and eternal love.
Bless him now and forever.

 Cheryl Barker

Praise Be to God

Let us bless and let us extol, let us tell aloud and let us raise aloft, let us set on high and let us honour, let us exalt and let us praise the Holy One — blessed be He! — though He is far beyond any blessing or song, any honour or any consolation that can be spoken of in this world.

Jewish Prayer

I asked for strength that I might achieve;
I was made weak that I might learn humbly to obey.

I asked for health that I might do greater things;
I was given infirmity that I might do better things.

I asked for riches that I might be happy;
I was given poverty that I might be wise.

I asked for power that I might have the praise of men;
I was given weakness that I might feel the need of God.

I asked for all things that I might enjoy life;
I was given life that I might enjoy all things.

I got nothing that I asked for,
but everything that I had hoped for.

Almost despite myself my unspoken prayers were answered;
I am, among all men, most richly blessed.

 Unknown Confederate Soldier

Blessings in Disguise

When our hearts are full
and our lives rich with blessings,
we sing praises to God.
How easy that is to do.
When our hearts are heavy
and our lives seem thick with remorse,
we cry out to God for help.
How easy that is to do.

The test of faith comes
when our hearts feel broken
and we turn to God in thanksgiving.
Not so easy to do.
But our souls are strengthened
as we live in faith, trusting in
the substance of things hoped for,
the evidence of things not seen.

Gratitude and faith help us
create a better experience of life.
We can come to honor every challenge
as a blessing in disguise,
and sing praises to God no matter what.

 Phylis Clay Sparks

Pray for the Little Things...

Help me to live this day quietly
   and easily;
To lean upon Thy great strength trustfully
   and restfully;
To wait for the unfolding of Thy will
   patiently and serenely;
To meet others peacefully and joyously;
And to face tomorrow confidently and
   courageously.

Anonymous

Any concern too small to be turned into a
prayer is too small to be made into a burden.

Corrie ten Boom

If for any wish thou darest not pray,
Then pray to God to cast that wish away.

Hartley Coleridge

☆ ☆ Pray for the Big... ☆ ☆

The midnight hour is a difficult period in a person's life.... No matter what midnight hour you're faced with, God can give you strength to live with it. Always remember that when you pray, God is working on your behalf. No matter what the midnight situation is, if you stay armed with prayer, God has a prescription for you. He will either remove it or give you the necessary strength to live through it. Therefore, rest in the knowledge that none of your prayers go unnoticed because through prayer you invoke God's power to work in your life.

☆ Reverend Bernice A. King

When what you are feeling
is simply too deep for words
and nothing anyone does or says
can provide you with the relief you need,
God understands.
He is your provider —
today, tomorrow, and always.
And He loves you.
Cast all of your cares on Him...
    and believe.

☆ Linda E. Knight

Rely on God's Love for Strength

When you rely on God's love,
  and come to Him in prayer,
  know that He will never
  leave you or ignore your needs.
In your weakness, God's strength
  can become your strength,
  when you lean upon the promises
  of His healing touch.

 Susan Hickman Sater

Prayer for worldly goods is worse than fruitless, but prayer for strength
of soul is that passion of the soul which catches the gift it seeks.

George Meredith

God grant me the strength
to reach out for my dreams
and see the world
with understanding and love,
and to believe in the beauty
of life and the dignity of mankind.

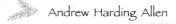 Andrew Harding Allen

This is my prayer to thee, my lord…
Strike at the root of penury in my heart.
Give me the strength lightly to bear my joys
 and sorrows.
Give me the strength to make my love fruitful
 in service.
Give me the strength never to disown the poor or
 bend my knees before insolent might.
Give me the strength to raise my mind high above
 daily trifles.
And give me the strength to surrender my strength
 to thy will with love.

 Rabindranath Tagore

These be our prayers — more strength, more light,
more constancy, more progress.

Do not pray for easy lives. Pray to be stronger men!
Do not pray for tasks equal to your powers. Pray for
powers equal to your tasks.

 Phillips Brooks

Pray for the World Around You

Love all God's creation, both the whole and every grain of sand. Love every leaf, every ray of light. Love the animals, love the plants, love each separate thing. If thou love each thing thou wilt perceive the mystery of God in all; and when once thou perceive this, thou wilt thenceforward grow every day to a fuller understanding of it: until thou come at last to love the whole world with a love that will then be all-embracing and universal.

Fyodor Dostoyevsky

The world is charged with the grandeur of God.

Gerard Manley Hopkins

He prayeth best, who loveth best
All things both great and small;
For the dear God who loveth us,
He made and loveth all.

Samuel Taylor Coleridge

A Buddhist Litany for Peace

As we are together, praying for Peace, let us be truly with each other.

Let us pay attention to our breathing.

Let us be relaxed in our bodies and our minds.

Let us return to ourselves and become wholly ourselves. Let us maintain a half-smile on our faces.

Let us be aware of the source of being common to us all and to all living things.

Evoking the presence of the Great Compassion, let us fill our hearts with our own compassion — towards ourselves and towards all living beings.

Let us pray that all living beings realize that they are all brothers and sisters, all nourished from the same source of life.

Let us pray that we ourselves cease to be the cause of suffering to each other.

Let us plead with ourselves to live in a way which will not deprive other living beings of air, water, food, shelter, or the chance to live.

With humility, with awareness of the existence of life, and of the sufferings that are going on around us, let us pray for the establishment of peace in our hearts and on earth.

Amen.

 The Venerable Thich Nhat Hahn

Our prayer is that men everywhere will learn finally to live as brothers, to respect each other's differences, to heal each other's wounds, to promote each other's progress, and to benefit from each other's knowledge.

 Adlai Stevenson

Evening Prayer

If I have wounded any soul today,
If I have caused one foot to go astray,
If I have walked in my own willful way —
      Good Lord, forgive!
If I have uttered idle words or vain,
If I have turned aside from want or pain,
Lest I myself should suffer through the strain —
      Good Lord, forgive!
If I have craved for joys that are not mine,
If I have let my wayward heart repine,
Dwelling on things of earth, not things divine —
      Good Lord, forgive!...
Forgive the sins I have confessed to Thee,
Forgive the secret sins I do not see,
That which I know not, Father, teach Thou me —
      Help me to live.

                ☆ Charles H. Gabriel

All that we ought to have thought and have not thought,
All that we ought to have said, and have not said,
All that we ought to have done, and have not done;

All that we ought not to have thought, and yet have thought,
All that we ought not to have spoken, and yet have spoken,
All that we ought not to have done, and yet have done;

For thoughts, words and works, pray we, O God, for forgiveness.

               ☆ From an Ancient Persian Prayer

There is hardly ever a complete silence in our soul. God is whispering to us wellnigh incessantly. Whenever the sounds of the world die out in the soul, or sink low, then we hear these whisperings of God. He is always whispering to us, only we do not always hear, because of the noise, hurry, and distraction which life causes as it rushes on.

 Frederick William Faber

Learn that the silence
Is God's way of pausing
So that we may hear
The voice of Faith.

 Corrine De Winter

Grant us grace, Almighty Father, so to pray as to deserve to be heard.

Jane Austen

I Prayed for You Today

I prayed for you today, gave thanks for your life, wished you the best, asked the heavens to bless you with good health and happiness. I sent you good thoughts, surrounded you with hope and faith and love. I asked your guardian angels to protect you and keep you safe from any harm and to blanket you with joy and contentment and peace and prosperity.

I asked that you be guided with the wisdom to make choices to enhance your life and the awareness to make changes that are in your best interest.

I wished for you a storehouse of opportunities, the ability to meet your goals, and the joy of your own approval and acceptance. I wished for you your heart's desire, every need met, every prayer answered, and every dream come true.

I asked that you be prepared for whatever life hands you or whatever you're going through. I asked that your spirit be strong and lead you and guide you each step of the way down every path you take. I asked the universe to confirm for you that you're someone very special. I asked the earth to be good to you, and I asked God to show you His perfect way. I prayed for you today.

Donna Fargo

Give Thanks to God

We thank Thee for this place in which we dwell; for the love that unites us; for the peace accorded us this day; for the hope with which we expect the morrow; for the health, the work, the food, and the bright skies that make our lives delightful.

 Robert Louis Stevenson

i thank You God for most this amazing
day:for the leaping greenly spirits of trees
and a blue true dream of sky;and for everything
which is natural which is infinite which is yes

(i who have died am alive again today,
and this is the sun's birthday;this is the birth
day of life and of love and wings:and of the gay
great happening illimitably earth)

how should tasting touching hearing seeing
breathing any—lifted from the no
of all nothing—human merely being
doubt unimaginable You?

(now the ears of my ears awake and
now the eyes of my eyes are opened)

 E. E. Cummings

We Thank Thee

For flowers that bloom about our feet,
Father, we thank Thee.
For tender grass so fresh, so sweet,
Father, we thank Thee.
For the song of bird and hum of bee,
For all things fair we hear or see,
Father in heaven, we thank Thee.

For blue of stream and blue of sky,
Father, we thank Thee.
For pleasant shade of branches high,
Father, we thank Thee.
For fragrant air and cooling breeze,
For beauty of the blooming trees,
Father in heaven, we thank Thee.

For this new morning with its light,
Father, we thank Thee.
For rest and shelter of the night,
Father, we thank Thee.
For health and food, for love and friends,
For everything Thy goodness sends,
Father in heaven, we thank Thee.

 Ralph Waldo Emerson

Through Prayer, You Are Never Alone

Prayer, when it is offered in the right way, redeems people from isolation. It assures them that they need not feel alone and abandoned. It lets them know that they are part of a greater reality, with more depth, more hope, more courage, and more of a future than any individual could have by himself. One goes to a religious service, one recites the traditional prayers, not in order to find God (there are plenty of other places where He can be found), but to find a congregation, to find people with whom you can share that which means the most to you. From that point of view, just being able to pray helps, whether your prayer changes the world outside you or not.

Harold S. Kushner

My every thought, my every action, is a moment in which divine support comes to me. I am never alone, never an exile, never a stranger from the heart of God. The heart of God holds me within its bountiful soil. I blossom there, rooted in faith, fed by the nutrients of divine love.

Julia Cameron

He Himself has said,
"I will never leave you
nor forsake you."

Hebrews 13:5 (NKJV)

God Is Here

God is here
   in the midst of a storm
to give you peace.
God is here during trials
   and temptations
to give you guidance.
God is here through turmoil
   and strife
to give you patience.
God is here among prejudice
   and hatred
to give you love.
God is here whenever things
   aren't going right
to give you hope.
God is here when you give up
   on your dreams
to give you faith.
At any time
and in any situation,
   you are never alone.
God is always here.

 Barbara Cage

A Prayer for the Gifts
God Has Given

Let us be thankful for
the blessings we receive.
Let us be thoughtful of others.
Let us remember dear and close friends.
Let us have faith in tomorrow.

Let us live life as a golden rule.
Let us find sunlight through the clouds.
Let us believe; let us be the people
we have the ability to be.
Let us have understanding.
Let us say this thanks, in prayer...

to God, for the gifts He has given.

Chris Gallatin

With each and every fear that you have
comes the opportunity to develop a deeper
faith, for God is always there waiting to lead
you to happiness, to love, to victory.

Donna Newman

May God Bless You

From His boundless wealth,
   may God bless you.
From His endless joy,
   may God fill you.
From the depth of His love,
   may God keep you
      throughout the coming years.

May God give you the gift
   of perfect wisdom
in every decision that you
   must make.

May a light fill your heart
   and confidence fill your soul
as you face life's challenges.
And may opportunities beyond any
   that you can imagine now
be only a prayer away
   as you entrust to God
each new tomorrow.

Linda E. Knight

ACKNOWLEDGMENTS

We gratefully acknowledge the permission granted by the following authors, publishers, and authors' representatives to reprint poems or excerpts from their publications.

Linda E. Knight for "There is no sorrow...." Copyright © 2000 by Linda E. Knight. All rights reserved. Reprinted by permission.

Word Publishing for "Have you heard God's voice?" from HOW TO BE BORN AGAIN by Billy Graham. Copyright © 1977 by Billy Graham. All rights reserved. Reprinted by permission of Word Publishing, Nashville, TN.

The University of Arkansas Press for "I had learned many years ago..." and "It's hard for us to accept..." from EVERYTHING TO GAIN by Jimmy and Rosalynn Carter. Copyright © 1987 and 1995 by Jimmy and Rosalynn Carter. All rights reserved. Reprinted by permission.

HarperCollins Publishers, Inc. for "Met a man today..." from WORDS I WISH I WROTE by Robert Fulghum. Copyright © 1997 by Robert Fulghum. All rights reserved. Reprinted by permission.

The University of Chicago Press for "Prayer does not change God..." by Sören Kierkegaard from THE PRAYERS OF KIERKEGAARD by P. F. Le Fevre. Copyright © 1956 by The University of Chicago Press. All rights reserved. Reprinted by permission.

PrimaDonna Entertainment Corp. for "Start Every Day with Prayer" and "I Prayed for You Today" by Donna Fargo. Copyright © 1999 by PrimaDonna Entertainment Corp. All rights reserved. Reprinted by permission.

Corrine De Winter for "Rising this morning..." and "Learn that the silence...." Copyright © 2000 by Corrine De Winter. All rights reserved. Reprinted by permission.

House of Cash for "My way of communicating with God..." from MAN IN BLACK by Johnny Cash, published by Zondervan Publishing House. Copyright © 1975 by Johnny Cash. All rights reserved. Reprinted by permission.

Barbara Cage for "A conversation with God...." Copyright © 2000 by Barbara Cage. All rights reserved. Reprinted by permission.

Scripture quotation marked NLT is taken from THE HOLY BIBLE, NEW LIVING TRANSLATION, published by Tyndale House Publishers, Inc. Copyright © 1996 by Tyndale House Publishers, Inc. All rights reserved.

Phylis Clay Sparks for "When our hearts are full...." Copyright © 1999 by Phylis Clay Sparks. All rights reserved. Reprinted by permission.

Broadway Books, a division of Random House, Inc., for "The midnight hour is a difficult period..." from HARD QUESTIONS, HEART ANSWERS by Bernice A. King. Copyright © 1996 by Bernice A. King. All rights reserved. Reprinted by permission.

Scribner, a division of Simon & Schuster, for "This is my prayer..." from GITANJALI by Rabindranath Tagore. Copyright © 1997 by Scribner. All rights reserved. Reprinted by permission.

Liveright Publishing Corporation for "i thank You God for most this amazing" from COMPLETE POEMS 1913-1962 by E. E. Cummings. Copyright © 1940 by E. E. Cummings. Copyright © 1968 by Marion Morehouse Cummings. All rights reserved. Reprinted by permission.

Schocken Books, a division of Random House, Inc., for "Prayer, when it is offered in the right way..." from WHEN BAD THINGS HAPPEN TO GOOD PEOPLE by Harold S. Kushner. Copyright © 1981 by Harold S. Kushner. All rights reserved. Reprinted by permission.

Jeremy P. Tarcher, a division of Penguin Putnam, Inc., for "My every thought..." from BLESSINGS: PRAYERS AND DECLARATIONS FOR A HEARTFUL LIFE by Julia Cameron. Copyright © 1998 by Julia Cameron. All rights reserved. Reprinted by permission.

A careful effort has been made to trace the ownership of poems used in this anthology in order to obtain permission to reprint copyrighted materials and give proper credit to the copyright owners. If any error or omission has occurred, it is completely inadvertent, and we would like to make corrections in future editions provided that written notification is made to the publisher:

SPS STUDIOS, INC., P.O. Box 4549, Boulder, Colorado 80306.

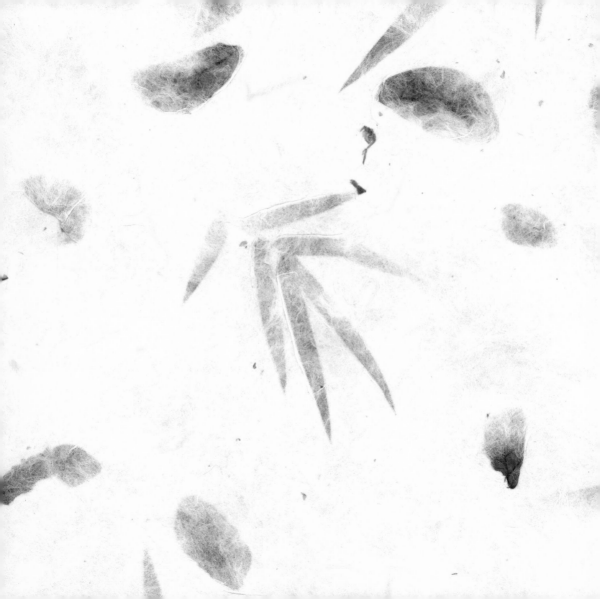